W9-BJF-014

Pebble™

My World
In My
Neighborhood

by Mari C. Schuh

Consulting Editor: Gail Saunders-Smith, PhD
Consultant: Susan B. Neuman, EdD
Former U.S. Assistant Secretary for Elementary
and Secondary Education
Professor, Educational Studies, University of Michigan

Capstone
press
Mankato, Minnesota

Pebble Books are published by Capstone Press,
151 Good Counsel Drive, P.O. Box 669, Mankato, Minnesota 56002.
www.capstonepub.com

Library of Congress Cataloging-in-Publication Data
Schuh, Mari C., 1975–
    In my neighborhood / by Mari C. Schuh.
    p. cm.—(Pebble Books. My world)
    Includes bibliographical references and index.
    ISBN-13: 978-0-7368-4239-6 (hardcover)   ISBN-10: 0-7368-4239-X (hardcover)
    ISBN-13: 978-0-7368-6117-5 (softcover)   ISBN-10: 0-7368-6117-3 (softcover)
    1. Neighborhood—Juvenile literature. 2. City and town life—Juvenile literature.
I. Title. II. Series: Pebble Books. My world (Mankato, Minn.)
HT152.S375 2006
307.3'362—dc22   2004030038
Summary: Simple text and photographs introduce basic community concepts
related to neighborhoods including location, things in a neighborhood, and different
types of neighborhoods.

Note to Parents and Teachers

The My World set supports national social studies standards related to
community. This book describes and illustrates neighborhoods. The images
support early readers in understanding the text. The repetition of words
and phrases helps early readers learn new words. This book also introduces
early readers to subject-specific vocabulary words, which are defined in the
Glossary section. Early readers may need assistance to read some words
and to use the Table of Contents, Glossary, Read More, Internet Sites, and
Index sections of the book.

Table of Contents

My Neighborhood

I live in a neighborhood. My house is on a street in my neighborhood.

My Neighborhood

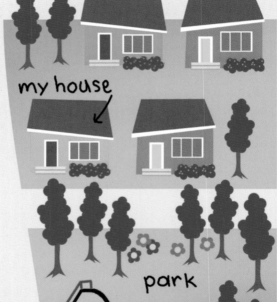

dentist →

school

my house

park

bakery

6

My neighborhood has
streets and homes.
It has a park
with a slide.

I play with friends
from my neighborhood.
They are my neighbors.

Neighborhood Places

My neighborhood
has stores.
My dad and I buy
bread at the bakery.

My neighborhood
has a school.
I go to school
with my friends.

FAMILY DENTAL

My neighborhood
has a dentist.
My mom takes me
to the dentist to have
my teeth cleaned.

16

Other Neighborhoods

Towns can have
many neighborhoods.
Neighborhoods can be
new or old.

18

Big cities,
like San Francisco,
have crowded
neighborhoods.

I live in a new
neighborhood.
What is your
neighborhood like?

Glossary

crowded—a lot of people packed together

neighborhood—a small area or section of a city or town where people live

neighbors—people who live near each other in the same neighborhood

street—a road in a city or town, often with sidewalks, houses, or other buildings along it

town—a group of neighborhoods that form a community; towns are smaller parts of a state.